The Power of...
by Z

A Guide to Achieving a Good and Happy Life
by Overcoming Its Challenges

SPOILERS PRESS
Hermosa Beach, CA

The Power of... by Z
© 2023 Pat Zartman

All rights reserved. This book or any portion thereof may not be reproduced or used in any manner whatsoever without the express written permission of the publisher except for the use of brief quotations in a book review.

Published by Spoilers Press, Hermosa Beach, CA

ISBN 978-0-9992510-8-9 (paperback)
ISBN 978-0-9992510-9-6 (ebook)

Book Design: Clarity Designworks

Printed in the United States of America

This book is dedicated to my wife, Sharkie,
my daughters, Teri and Chrissie,
and all of the students and athletes with whom
I have had the pleasure to teach and coach.

Contents

About the Author vii
Introduction ix
The Power of Choice 1
The Power of Purpose 5
The Power of Doing More. 7
The Power of Always Being There. 9
The Power of Passion. 11
The Power of Persistence. 13
The Power of Now 17
The Power of Attitude 19
The Power of Best / Improve 21
The Power of Patience 23
The Power of "Can Do" 25
The Power of Determination 27
The Power of Kindness 29
The Power of Planning / Preparation 31
The Power of Knowledge 33
The Power of Will. 35
The Power of Focus / Concentration. 37
The Power of Enthusiasm 39

The Power of Accountability / Responsibility 41
The Power of Grit 43
The Power of Adapting 45
The Power of Self-Discipline 47
The Power of Optimism 49
The Power of Effort 51
The Power of the Truth and Honesty 53
The Power of Belief 55
The Power of Intensity 57
The Power of Hope 59
The Power of Diligence 61
The Power of Resilience 63
The Power of Experience 65
The Power of Laughter 67
The Power of Talent and Skills 69
The Power of Skills 71
The Power of Caring 73
The Power of Gratitude 75
The Power of Courage 77
The Power of Expectancy 79
The Power of Endurance 81
The Power of Teamwork 83
The Power of Commitment 85
The Power of Consistency 87
The Power of Love 89
The Power of Fulfillment 91
Final Thoughts 93
Special Thanks 95

About the Author

Who is Z? Z is Pat Zartman. He is a noted history and psychology teacher and also a football, volleyball and strength training coach. Pat is well known for the life lessons imparted both in the classroom and in the competitive arena.

In volleyball, his athletes earned All-State and All-American Honors and won State, National and World Championships and Olympic Gold. Pat has written articles and contributed to magazines and books at both the domestic and international levels. He has also done coaching and player clinics in the United States and abroad. He has been inducted into the Southern California Indoor Volleyball Hall of Fame.

Introduction

During the past several years, we have been faced with serious health, environmental, political and social challenges. They have brought out the best in many, but some frightening ideas have been developed and embraced during this time.

Through the media and advertising, people are being taught that they are victims, that they are inadequate, and that they are not responsible for their lives. They are being taught that: "I am entitled to everything," that "I deserve everything," and that "I am owed everything." This creates unrealistic expectations, disappointment, fear, anger and a sense of powerlessness.

The truth is that humans are goal-striving mechanisms. Our country is based on the foundations of rugged individualism, individual initiative, a strong work ethic, and a "can do" attitude. Our forefathers came to this country seeking a better life and were willing to work for it. They worked hard, and many got that life. Others wanted more, and moved to the frontier willing to conquer the unknown in order to reach their goals.

We have life stories of people like Andrew Carnegie who came to the United States as a poor immigrant, and through hard work and frugal living, became one of the richest men in the world. We have the novels of Horatio Alger telling about poor boys who became rich and successful through hard work and careful living. Jacob Riis, a New York City newspaper reporter, wrote articles pointing out that though it was truly terrible that people had to live the in slums and alleys in New York City, many moved up and out as did the ones before them. The German rag picker became a rich business man. The Irish hod carrier became a bricklayer. The Italian beggar soon owned his own fruit stand and then a fruit company. Freed men took advantage of land grant acts, many went west, and some became successful farmers and ranchers.

Success, happiness, and satisfaction came from achieving goals. This is available to all of us. We have POWERS that are *free* and *available* to all of us that can lead us to the achievement of all of our personal goals.

WHAT ARE THESE POWERS?

The Power of Choice

DECISIONS, OPPORTUNITY

"The quality of your choices dictate the quality of your life."
— HAROLD MORRIS

The choices you make every day from what you wear, to what you eat, to what you do create opportunities, and they carve out and determine who you are and what you will be. They have a tremendous impact on your life.

One morning I arrived at my classroom at about 6:30 A.M. to get ready for my 7 A.M. peer counseling class. Standing at the door was a tall, muscular police officer wearing mirrored sunglasses with a middle-aged man whom he introduced as Harold Morris. The officer said that our district had sent Morris to speak to my class.

After taking roll, I introduced Mr. Morris to the class, and he began to tell his life story.

He said that he came from a dysfunctional family, grew up on the streets, and had no friends and no one who cared for him. He turned to a life of crime. He robbed stores and in the process killed several people. He was eventually captured and sentenced to life in prison without parole.

While in prison, he killed three fellow inmates and was put in solitary confinement for life. He was confined to his cell except for a thirty minute period in the exercise yard each day that was enclosed by electrified, barbed wire fences overseen by a tower guard with a rifle. During that time, he sat on a bench and smoked cigarettes.

One day, a young boy walking by threw a ball into the yard. He called to Morris to throw it back. Cursing, Harold threw it as far as he could. The boy came back, and kept coming back until he got Morris to play catch with him daily. This went on for several years until one day when the boy was not there, and did not return.

Harold Morris found himself alone again. He missed the boy. He was the only person in Harold's life who was a friend and there for him.

Several years passed, and one day his jailer told Morris that he was retiring in a month and that Harold would have a new jailer. When that time came, Harold was introduced to a tall, muscular young man, his new jailer. That man asked him if he recognized him. Morris said that he didn't.

It turned out that his new jailer was the boy with whom he had played catch. He had gone away to school, became a police officer, got a job at the prison, and now had become Harold's Jailer. He worked with the prison and the prison board until he was allowed to take Morris around the country to talk to students and relay his message.

His message was: Make bad choices (robbery and murder) and bad things happen to you. Make good choices (the boy) and good things happen to you.

Another impactful message can be learned regarding choices:

A man moved to New York City where he got several job offers. He called his parents for advice, and they recommended taking the highest paying job. He weighed the pros and cons of the offers, and finally chose the lowest paying job which was the one he liked the best.

Six months later, 9/11 occurred. If he had taken the job recommended by his parents, he would have been in a building in which 658 employees died. Often when making choices, the outcome is unknown.

Yes, the quality of your choices do dictate the quality of your life.

So...CHOOSE WELL!

The Power of Purpose

AN INTENTION OR AIM: A REASON FOR DOING SOMETHING

"He who has a WHY can endure any How."
— FREDERICK NIETZCHE

It has been said that there are two great days in a person's life—The day he is born, and the day he discovers WHY. The "WHY" is his purpose.

An automobile without an engine is useless. Without the driving mechanism, the vehicle is not capable of movement. The power of purpose is the driving force. Without purpose, an individual can never reach his full potential or accomplish what he set his mind on. Purpose is the engine to the automobile, the flame to the oven, the electricity to the lamp, the light to the lighthouse.

A sense of purpose enables you to focus. It can help you achieve your goals and give meaning to your life. It is a source of energy, motivation, and direction.

Having purpose in life can extend it, and give it excitement and stability. It can make you happier and more energetic.

Purpose can change at different ages, stages and times of life.

NOW is the time to find your purpose!

The Power of Doing More

GOING THE EXTRA MILE:
ACHIEVING SUCCESS OVER AND OVER
ABOVE THE STANDARD EXPECTATION.

"In order to be a success, in order to be great, all you have to do is a little bit more that what is asked of you because everyone else is content to just get by."
— OG MANDINO

You do not have to do something great in order to exceed expectations, because even the smallest task counts toward creating something big. Any big success can be credited to doing a little extra work as is often seen in the accomplishments of athletes, musicians, and C.E.O.S.

"The difference between ordinary and extraordinary is that little extra."
— JIMMY JOHNSON

I had the opportunity to coach two young men in football who were strong, agile, and quick. They worked hard and played hard and both earned All-League and All-C.I.F. Honors. One was six foot and three inches tall and weighed two hundred and fifteen pounds. The other was five foot and seven inches and weighed one hundred and fifty-five pounds. They both were defensive tackles. How did the smaller one do it? Each day after a hard practice and conditioning he would come to me and ask: "Coach, can you give me a ten? (minutes) He used that time to improve his skill and techniques on a daily basis. It worked!

Likewise, Jackie Silva, The first Olympic Gold Medalist in Women's Beach Volleyball, would ask me to drill her on skills that she felt needed improvement. She would yell "Pat Zartman, Again, Again, Again!" until she was satisfied with her performance. Her desire to win, for perfection, and to be great were relentless. Her Gold Medal attests to that.

When, at the end of the day, was the last time you asked your boss: "Is there anything else that I can do before I leave?" At home before leaving, did you ask a parent or spouse: "Is there anything that I can do before I go?"

Doing more is something that everyone should strive for. It builds character, and makes you feel good about who you are and what you are doing with your life. It also can help you achieve your goals. Nothing truly important has ever been done without hard work and extra effort.

Always do a little bit more

The Power of Always Being There

THE SIMPLE ACT OF OFFERING YOUR PRESENCE, CARE AND LOVE IN SUPPORT OF ANOTHER

During my forty-seven years of teaching psychology, my favorite assignment was to have students identify the most important/significant person in their lives. Forty-five times the winners were Mom; the other two were Dad. Why? It was because moms were *always there* for them.

Always being there is more important than most people think. It has a huge impact on individuals. Showing people around us that we consistently care can make all of the difference to them. Sometimes all that people need is your presence. People need the reassurance that they are not alone.

Always being there is not just a little thing. It can make all of the difference.

Who are you always there for?

The Power of Passion

DESIRE, ENTHUSIASM, EXCITEMENT

*"There is no passion to be found in playing small—
in settling for a life that is less than
you are capable of living."*
— HARRIET TUBMAN

"A little fire gives little heat; a big fire gives big heat."

*"Passion is energy. Feel the power that comes
from focusing on what excites you."*
— ANTHONY D-ANGELO

Passion refers to a natural urge or desire to commit to something that is important to you. It motivates you to work for your goals. It fuels your life. It provides the happiness generated from doing what you love.

Passionate people put passion into everything that they do. It creates enthusiasm and motivation to help them achieve their goals.

What is your passion?

The Power of Persistence

NEVER GIVING UP:
THE FIRM OR OBSTINATE CONTINUANCE
IN A GIVEN COURSE OF ACTION
IN SPITE OF DIFFICULTY OR OPPOSITION

"Persistence = Success"

There are times in our lives when we just want to give up. We feel that it is not worth it to continue to fight.

STOP!

As Thomas Edison said: "Many of life's failures are people who did not realize how close they were to success when they gave up." No matter how many times you fall, all that matters in the end is how many times you get up."

Thomas Edison did not invent the light bulb on his first or second try. It took over 10,000 times to succeed. Michael Jordan was not an overnight sensation. He was cut from his high school basketball team, he missed more than 9,000 shots, he lost almost 300 games and he missed the winning shot on 26 occasions. Yet he is considered one of the greatest basketball players of all time. Abraham Lincoln lost many elections including a bid for the Senate and a Nomination for Vice President. He was elected President of the United States and is considered one of the best Presidents in our national history.

I met a girl named Sharkie who is an exceptional person. She is smart, witty, caring, energetic, attractive and athletic. She came to me one day and asked if I would be her volleyball coach. Over the next couple of years our team became successful, Sharkie became an outstanding player, and we became close friends.

As time went on, I developed deep feelings for her, but there was an eight year age gap between us, and she had a boyfriend. Eventually, she and her boyfriend broke up, and I started to date her. We shared the same interests and values and always had a great time together. She was my best friend, and I was in love with her.

One evening I asked her to marry me. Shocked, she immediately said : "NO!" We continued to see each other but also dated others. Time went on, and again we were seeing each other exclusively. It seemed that the time was right, so I proposed again. Her response was: "NO, and don't ever ask me again." (Ouch, that hurt deeply.) My response was: "I am going to ask you one more time. If you say no, I'll never see you again."

Months passed. I never got the chance to ask her again because one evening eight years after I met her, Sharkie told her parents and me that she and I were going to be married. Her Dad looked at me, smiled and asked: "Is that okay with you Pat?" We got married in 1976 and are still married and in love.

Persistence plays a critical role in the quest for wisdom, achievement, fulfillment, and self-confidence. In order to achieve what one sets out to do, one needs to push past obstacles despite how difficult they are. Sheldon Newton, motivational speaker, states that: "Persistence is what makes one succeed where others have failed. When one individual makes up his mind to accomplish a particular feat and sets his focus in that direction refusing to be deterred, he usually gets what he went after."

Life strategist Gary Coxe points out that: "There is no substitute for being persistent. It is the key to success." Thus, no great achievement is possible without persistent work.

Never, ever, ever give up!

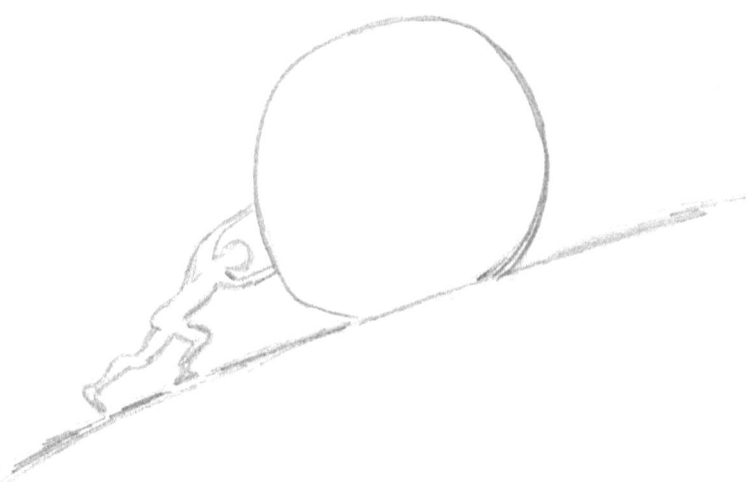

The Power of Now

THE PRESENT MOMENT

> *"Yesterday is history, tomorrow is a mystery, today is a gift. That is why we call it the present."*
> — BILL KEANE

Living in the past can create feelings of pain, regret, and sadness. Living for the future can create worry, anxiety and stress. If you live in the now, you will no longer be controlled by negative emotions, but instead you will find peace within yourself. Without the Power of the Now, you are bound to your past with no means of improving your future.

In order to find happiness and prevent stress, you must live in the now. By being able to live in the moment, it enables you to grow and find joy in your daily life. It helps you to find inner bliss by making you conscious, healthy, and happy.

Matt Mayberry, a motivational speaker, tells us that "We must have a vision of where we want to go and take ownership of where we currently are, but something that we can't let happen is to neglect the present." He goes on to tell us that "the present is here to help mold us into the individuals that we need to become."

All achievements and all accomplishments occur in the Now. Now is all that we really have, and as an author and motivational speaker Leo Buscaglia has said: "If not now, when?"

Make every moment count!

The Power of Attitude

A WAY OF RESPONDING
TO PEOPLE AND SITUATIONS

"You change your future by changing your attitude."
— OPRAH WINFREY

Your attitude has a huge impact on your life. It becomes manifest through your behavior. It is not only our beliefs, but also how we act in accordance with those beliefs. Attitude is a combination of how we think and how we act.

It has been said that success is 85% attitude and 15% knowledge.

Our attitude has a huge impact on our life. It affects our physical health, our enthusiasm, our confidence, and our success. It creates possibilities. It drives behaviors. The more positive value that you see in life, the happier you become and the more you enjoy life.

Anyone can learn to have a positive attitude. Actor Christine Taylor says that "A person with a positive attitude is someone who is proactive, who finds a desire within himself to create positive change." She continues by giving the example of a person in a wheelchair looking at a staircase. Anyone would be frustrated in this situation. The difference is that a person with a positive attitude would do something about it—he would find another alternative.

Having a positive attitude is a choice. You need to see your life as a series of simple choices. You have the power to change your life simply by choosing to have a positive attitude.

The ancient Greeks said to "Look for the good." And it was implied that you would find it. Conversely, look for the bad and guess what, you will find it. Thus our attitude toward life determines life's attitude toward us.

Attitude = Outcome

The Power of Best / Improve

*"The real test:
Did I make my best effort on every play?"*
— BUD WILKENSON

Bud Wilkenson, football coach at Oklahoma, holds the N.C.A.A. record for the most consecutive wins by any major division football coach at 47 in a row.

As a young football coach, I had the opportunity to attend a football clinic that had Bud Wilkerson as the keynote speaker. I was going to be able to learn techniques, drills and plays from one of the best.

When we got to the convention site, I went directly to the room assigned to him. I sat in the front row with my notebook and pencil. I skipped the other speakers and waited there until Coach Wilkerson's time arrived.

As the time drew near, the room was filled to capacity and overflowed into the hall.

As his talk began, Coach said that if you were interested in techniques or drills, there was another coach down the hall who had great ones. He said that he didn't have many. If you were interested in special plays, there was another coach who had some great ones in another room down the hall. He said that he really didn't have any.

I was shocked and disappointed.

But then he said: "If you want to know how we have been so consistently able to win, then stay here and I'll tell you.

YES!

Coach Wilkenson said that he demanded one thing of his players. He demanded that every time that they stepped onto the field for practice or for a game that they always did their best and tried to improve on their last performance. In doing so there is no pressure.

Some teams lose because they look past supposed weak teams. Some teams lose because they fear supposedly stronger and more powerful teams. But if you always do your best trying to improve, winning usually takes care of itself.

This philosophy applies to all aspects of your life. Make a commitment to yourself to:

Always do your best, and try to improve on your last performance in everything that you do.

The Power of Patience

THE ABILITY OR WILLINGNESS TO
SUPPRESS RESTLESSNESS OR ANNOYANCE WHEN
CONFRONTED WITH DELAY

"Patience is the best remedy for every trouble."
— PLAUTUS

In other words, patience is the capacity to accept or to tolerate trouble and suffering without getting angry or upset. It gives you the time to evaluate situations before you make decisions.

A story by Ratilautu Sigh tells of a King who required a test for those who wanted to be his personal assistant. They were told that if they filled a pot with water from a small pond, that the job would be theirs. However, they were also told that there was a big hole in the pot. Some did not try, some tried and failed and gave up. But one kept filling the pot even though the water kept flowing out. He continued until the pond was empty. There in the mud he found a diamond ring and gave it to the King. The King said that the ring was his reward for patience and hard work. He also said that the man had proved fit for the job as his personal assistant and that the job was his.

No one has ever achieved anything without being patient to some extent. Dr. Martin Luther King Jr. did not reach his goal of desegregation without having to wait patiently for legislation to be passed. Life-style writer Susan McQuillein states that: "Patience is valuable for coping with long lines, being put on hold, or interacting with disagreeable people." Whether you are dealing with a two hour wait to get on an amusement park ride, waiting for a customer service representative to get on the phone with you, or having to deal with an irate boss, it would be impossible for you to calmly move through those situations without some degree of patience. Having patience can save you from making bad decisions. It can help you master any art, enhance and shape talents and skills, and overcome challenges. It can contribute to happiness and health. According to Bo Jackson: "Baseball is easy if you've got patience, and Football is easy if you understand patience."

Patience Is Power

The Power of "Can Do"

THE ABILITY AND WILLINGNESS TO ACCEPT AND MEET CHALLENGES

"If you think you can do a thing, or think you can't do a thing, you are right."
— HENRY FORD

"Don't let what you cannot do interfere with what you can do."
— JOHN WOODEN

Many years ago I read a story by Brad Lemley in *Parade Magazine* about a man named W. Mitchel. Lemley tells us that Mitchell's face was a patchwork of multicolored skin grafts, the fingers of his hands were either missing or mere stubs, and his paralyzed legs were thin and useless.

What happened to him? He had been horrifically burned and nearly killed in a freak motorcycle accident, and then four years later, paralyzed from the waist down in an airplane crash.

Yet Mitchell became a millionaire, a respected environmentalist, a sought-after speaker, a former mayor and congressional candidate, a happy husband, and even a river rafter and sky diver. And he became all of these things after his accidents.

W. Mitchell has said that his life proves that all limitations are self-imposed. He added that it is not what happens to you in life, it's what you do about it. He added that he could have chosen to see his situation as a setback or a starting point. During his rehab, Mitchell realized that before the accidents, there were 10,000 things that he could do. After, there were 9,000. He could spend the rest of his life dwelling on the 1,000 that he lost, but he chose to focus on the 9,000 that were left. He said that he had two big bumps in his life, but he chose to not use them as an excuse to quit.

This story shows that with a "Can Do" approach, you enter a situation already knowing that you will be able to succeed. You are able to take action because you are comfortable in knowing that you have the chance to succeed. It allows you to achieve great things because you truly believe that you can. It uplifts you and guides you to success. It benefits every aspect of your life by helping you to find ways to solve problems by focusing on finding solutions rather than obstacles. Your "Can Do" mindset is extremely important because it can be the difference between getting what you want or not getting what you want. A "Can Do Attitude" will keep you positive and optimistic. You will be more inclined to pursue your goals and dreams and to reach them.

You can do it!

The Power of Determination

NOT GIVING UP NO MATTER WHAT

"Our greatest glory is not in never falling, but is rising every time we fall."
— CONFUCIUS

Determination is the word that keeps us from staying down on the ground. Determination is a characteristic that makes people get back up nine times when they have fallen eight. In life, we will reach road blocks, and we will hit rock bottom. It will hurt, and in these moments, we may want to rage, quit, or cry. However, how we choose to deal with those situations will dictate the quality of our success.

When we are so close to giving up, determination keeps us running. It is important to realize that adversity is unavoidable. If there were no problems in the world, life would be just as exciting as watching paint dry. It is easy to throw in the towel when you have failed multiple times. Remember that you haven't failed until you've stopped trying. The will to push through all of the negative barriers, the will to stick with it, the will to strive for nothing less than your aspirations…that is where true success comes from.

Many people talk about wanting to achieve their goals: lose weight, gain muscle, become phenomenal in a sport. However, most falter when it comes to sacrificing. To be great, you have to give a little. Being determined to achieve your dreams means having to set aside some other things while you are in pursuit of them. For example, when it comes to losing weight, push through lazy thoughts, get off the couch, and start eating sensibly and start exercising. Many people who talk about their goals, lack the willingness to get started on achieving them.

With determination, anything is possible. This is shown in the life of Glenn Cunningham. At the age of seven, he was badly burned in a schoolhouse fire. He barely survived and was not expected to ever walk again. By sheer determination, he overcame his adversity and became a runner. He was a sensation in the mile run both in high school and in college. Glenn became a two-time Olympian and Medalist, and a World Record Holder in the Mile. He went against all of the odds to become a Track Legend. He did not care what other people thought he couldn't do. He knew what he wanted, and he worked for it despite how difficult it was.

Your mind's strength is determined to the extent you work against the odds and succeed. The willingness to do what is necessary to achieve one's dream is the major element that helps you push through hardships.

Always having that drive to do what is necessary to achieve your dreams is difficult. That is why it is rewarded with something sweet—success. It is important to note the fact that the longer you hang on, and the more you push, the more likely it is that you will achieve your goals. Through determination all things are possible.

Never Say Never.

The Power of Kindness

BEING FRIENDLY, GENEROUS, CONSIDERATE, CARING, AND HELPFUL.

> *"Three things in human life are important:*
> *First is to be kind,*
> *second is to be kind,*
> *and third is to be kind."*
> — HENRY JAMES

The smallest act of kindness has the potential to turn a life around. This can be seen in the story of a woman who lost her baby when its heart stopped beating during the fourth month of her pregnancy. She was devastated, and nervous about returning to school as a middle school teacher. How could she face the kids? After four weeks of recovering, she walked into her empty classroom and turned on the lights. Glued to the walls were 100 colored paper butterflies. Each had a handwritten message on it from current and former students. Each of them had encouraging messages on them for her. It was exactly what she needed. — *Jennifer Garcia-Esquival*

Kindness deepens the spirit and produces rewards that cannot be completely explained. A simple random act of kindness can inspire others to pay if forward. It triggers a chain reaction of people being kind to others.

Overall, kindness is a valuable virtue that influences, changes and impacts every living human being. It is the core of our humanity and the light that brings us hope. Kindness is an elixir to us for a happy life. Be the reason someone smiles.

Be kind.

The Power of Planning / Preparation

PLANNING LETS YOU *KNOW* WHAT YOU WILL BE DOING WHEREAS PREPARATION GETS YOU READY FOR WHAT YOU WILL BE DOING.

PLANNING
Forethought; ability to anticipate the consequences of your actions and the actions of others; thinking about and organizing activities required to achieve a desired goal.

"As in all successful ventures, the foundation is planning."
— EARL NIGHTENGALE

Individuals who take the time to determine what they want to achieve in life are much more likely to accomplish their goals and objectives than those who leave their lives to chance.

Examples of planning are seen in team sports. Coaches scout opponents, and then develop a strategy that gives them the best chance to win.

Having a plan in order provides you with the ability to have a path of action ready for the given situation. It gives you the ability, not to eliminate risk, but to increase the odds of success. You have a strategy in place for doing things before they need to be done. This contributes to your mental and physical health by reducing stress and building confidence. It enhances your ability to accomplish your most important and desired goals.

Planning facilitates success.

PREPARATION
The act of getting ready to do something

"By failing to prepare, you are preparing to fail."
— BEN FRANKLIN

Confucius once claimed that: "Success depends upon previous preparation, and that without such preparation that there is sure to be failure." Thus the quality of your preparation decides the quality of your performance.

By preparing for what is to come in the future, you will be able to take on anything that comes your way. Being prepared for opportunities allows you to succeed, and the more time and effort you put into preparing for the future, the bigger and brighter your opportunities will be.

Preparation is an essential aspect in the real world. For example, when couples plan to have a baby, they take preparation classes to help them reduce anxiety and to provide coping techniques to help with pain management.

Business Psychologist Camille Preston says that: "Preparation is about planning proactively rather than responding reactively." It is one of the key ingredients in success and happiness. It betters performances, achievements, and lives.

Success comes from preparation.

The Power of Knowledge

FACTS, INFORMATION, AND SKILL
ACQUIRED BY A PERSON THROUGH
EXPERIENCE OR EDUCATION

"Knowledge is power if you know how to use it."
— DENISE CARUSO

What you don't know is the source of your greatest unhappiness. A lack of knowledge keeps you from your goals.

A story tells of a giant ship engine failure. The owner brought in many experts, but none could fix it. Finally he brought in an old man who had been fixing ships since he was a boy. He inspected the engine, grabbed a hammer, and tapped something. Instantly the engine started to run. It was fixed. A week later the owner received an itemized bill from the old man for ten thousand dollars. It read: Tapping with hammer $2.00 and knowing where to tap: $9,998.

Knowledge helps you to understand what you encounter. The more that you know about things, the easier it is to grasp their meaning. It gives you a chance to process things much faster and more accurately than others. The knowledge that you have determines the decisions that you make. Knowledge gives you options, and these options give you power.

Knowledge Is Power.

The Power of Will

THE ABILITY TO RESIST SHORT TERM TEMPTATIONS IN ORDER TO MEET LONG TERM GOALS AND THE ENERGETIC DETERMINATION OF CONTROL EXERTED TO DO SOMETHING OR RESTRAIN IMPULSES.

Vince Lombardi said: "It's the will to win, the will to excel. These are the things that endure, and they are far more important than any of the events that occasion them." He added that "The difference between a successful person and others isn't a lack of strength, not a lack of knowledge, but rather a lack of will."

Everyone despite size or strength, has the ability to overcome obstacles and achieve goals through willpower. It is something that one must never underestimate because it allows a person to accomplish amazing things. As Christopher Reeve has said: "So many of our dreams seem impossible, then they seem probable, and then when we summon the Will, they soon become inevitable." Willpower gives you the strength to keep going when you are physically, mentally, and emotionally spent. An English Proverb says: "Where there's a will, there's a way," and Olympian Roger Banister tells us that: "A man who can drive himself further once effort gets painful is the man who will win."

An example of this is people who quit smoking or overcome addictions "cold turkey." They decide to stop, and by the power of their Will, they hold their desires in check and withstand physical and mental withdrawals and they break their habit.

Willpower allows us to resist short-term temptations, and to achieve both short-term and long-term goals. It is an essential factor in changing habits and lifestyles. It is correlated with positive life outcomes such as higher self-esteem, lower substance abuse rates, greater financial security, improved physical and mental health, and overall success. With willpower you are bestowed with an inner strength.

Will it!

The Power of Focus / Concentration

INVESTING YOURSELF TOTALLY INTO THE TASK AT HAND WITHOUT DISTRACTIONS.

"The powers of the mind are like the rays of the sun. When they are concentrated, they illuminate."
— SWAMI VIVEKANANDA

By centering your attention on a single stimulus, it allows you to perform your task to the best of your ability. The more focused you are, the more successful you can be at whatever you do. It allows you to put your full and total effort into achieving your goal. Bruce Lee told us that: "The successful warrior is the average man with laser focus," and Vince Lombardi told us that: "Success demands singleness of purpose." Billy Chapel in the movie, *For the Love of the Game*, locks in and eliminates outside pressures through concentration.

William Allman in his book, *The Mental Edge*, says that athletes, musicians and dancers enter the ZONE (Lock in, the Flow, Stream of Consciousness) when they become totally engrossed in activity. With full concentration on one thing at a time, we advance in the world. In order to produce at your peak level, you need to work for extended periods on a single task free from distractions. According to author Og Mandino, it is being in this state that can lead to excellence in any field. It can improve memory, mental performance and will power. It can help us to achieve more and to do so more efficiently.

By focusing on the moment, we are able to eliminate everything but the *Now*, and it is in the *Now* that all things are accomplished. Actor Dwane Johnson, also know as *The Rock*, has said that "success at anything comes down to this: focus and effort, and we control both."

Your focus And concentration determine your reality.

The Power of Enthusiasm

STRONG EXCITEMENT
OF FEELING ABOUT SOMETHING

"Nothing great was ever achieved without enthusiasm."
— RALPH WALDO EMERSON

When you are enthusiastic, it makes you more authentic, and it gives you the courage and perseverance to achieve your goals. It is not how or when we accomplish something that matters most, it is the sense of enthusiasm during the process that demonstrates our quality of life. Happiness is a direct result of enthusiasm. Enthusiasm keeps you focused, gives you energy and the motivation to take action, helps you push through life's challenges and difficulties, and inspires you. It is infectious and contagious.

This brings to mind a story of a group of people standing in line for over an hour waiting for service. They were becoming more and more impatient, disgruntled and angry. At that point a little boy ran from his mother to another woman who asked him how old he was. The boy help up two fingers and said, Two!" His mother then said, "How old are you?" He raised three fingers and yelled "THREE!" He became excited, and started running around the room yelling "THREE, THREE! THREE!" with a big smile on his face. Soon, this show of enthusiasm became infectious, and the people in the room started to smile, then laugh, and then talk to one another. This enthusiasm of a little boy had caused a change in the attitude of those waiting in line.

Enthusiasm is the greatest skill that we can develop. It changes everything. It is the greatest asset in the world. All you need to be really happy is to have something to be enthusiastic about.

Have enthusiasm for everything that you do.

The Power of Accountability / Responsibility

ACCOUNTABILITY
Taking responsibility for decisions made and actions taken and accepting the consequences of those actions.

> *"Accountability means to say what you do and do what you say."*
> — P. ZHU

Rob Liano, author and life coach, states that: "If you think someone or something other than yourself is responsible for your happiness or success, I'd guess that you're not that happy or successful." Accountability is crucial because it molds a person into becoming more responsible, positive, and in charge of his life through the choices that he makes.

Mark Manson, self-help author, tells us that "Nobody else is ever responsible for your situation but you." Many people may be to blame for your unhappiness, but nobody is ever responsible for your unhappiness but you. This is because you always get to choose how you see thing, how you react to things, and how you value things. You always get to choose the metric by which to measure your experiences." Accountability is essential in life because we have the power to either make something good out of a given situation or just give up.

RESPONSIBILITY
Accepting that you are fully in charge of your successes and failures

"Accept responsibility for your life, know that it is you who will get you where you want to go, no one else."
— LES BROWN

When you realize that you are in charge of your own experiences, true growth begins and new experiences arise. You will be able to take full ownership of your successes and that will make you more controlled, confident, direct, and passionate. To begin the journey of accepting personal responsibility, you must accept the idea that you are in charge of your own life.

According to motivational speaker Hal Erod:
"The moment you accept the responsibility for everything in your life is the moment that you gain the power to change anything in your life."

Responsibility empowers you. If you are responsible for yourself, you will no longer be dependent on others. You will be fully in charge of your life. As Harry Browne tells us in his book, *How I Found Freedom in an Unfree World*:

"There is no freedom without responsibility." Thus, if you are not in charge of your life, then someone else is.

Responsibility creates freedom.

The Power of Grit

UNYIELDING COURAGE IN THE
FACE OF HARDSHIP OF DANGER:
TENACITY: TOUGHNESS

"Never give up no matter what"
— LOUIE ZAMPERINI

Grit allow us to overcome the obstacles that face us by maintaining our strength as an individual. It allows us to remain optimistic in the face of adversity with a resolve to make things better. Grit allows us to push through hard situations and face adversity with confidence regardless of the circumstances. This inner strength and courage also contribute to our overall happiness and confidence.

One famous example is the story of Louie Zamperini. He was a famous mile runner in high school and college and an Olympian. He also became famous for his survival at sea as well as his survival as a prisoner of war.

In high school, he set national records for his times in the mile race. Louie became famous for his ability to dig deep and have a ferocious "kick on the last lap." He was able to do that because he heeded his older brother's preaching that: "Isn't one minute of pain worth a lifetime of glory?"

While in college, during an N.C.A.A. Track Meet, Louie's competitors boxed him in so that he could not pass them. In the process, his shin was gashed by an opponent's spikes and a rib was fractured by another's elbow. Gasping for air, and with his sock filling with blood, Louie remained resolute. He finally broke free and finished the race ahead of the pack. Not only had he won, but he had also broken the men's national collegiate record for the mile race.

Having competed in the Olympics while in high school, Louie's future Olympic Dreams were interrupted by the Second World War.

Louie and the members of his crew were shot down while searching the ocean for a downed American air craft. He survived for forty-seven days at sea through grit and determination. He finally washed ashore, but was captured by the Japanese who physically and mentally abused and tortured him on a daily basis for more than two years. Louie's grit and toughness had prepared him for the agonies he faced as a prisoner of war where he endured regular beatings, threats of death, brutality, dehumanization and starvation rations.

As Louie said:

"Never give up no matter what."

The Power of Adapting

BEING ABLE TO ADJUST TO NEW CONDITIONS

> *"It is not the strongest of the species that survives, nor the most intelligent. It is the one that is most adaptable to change."*
> — CHARLES DARWIN

Adapting may be the most difficult part of living. The reason is that we often get comfortable or stuck in situations that keep us from reaching our goals. An old adage says that if it ain't broke, don't fix it. However, if you are not succeeding, you need to fix it.

In weight-training athletes often improve to a point, but then plateau out. No matter how hard they work, they are stuck and do not improve. They have developed a routine that has set limits. Never fear, the confusion principle is here. It tells us that to improve, we must change the routine by increasing weight, or using fewer sets and reps, or by reducing weight with more sets and reps.

Adapting helps you to live, thrive and survive in a changing world. It helps you to make the plans necessary to handle change. Learning to successfully navigate through change is key. Motivational speaker, Jim Rohn says that: "Your life does not get better by choice, it gets better by change." It gives you a greater opportunity to get what you want and what you need. It leads to success, satisfaction, greater well-being and a happier life.

Adapting is key.

The Power of Self-Discipline

THE ABILITY TO MAKE YOURSELF DO THINGS THAT SHOULD BE DONE

"With self-discipline most anything is possible."
— PLATO

Self-discipline is a continuous effort. It is a habit and the foundation for success. It gives you the power and inner strength to follow through on whatever you do. It is the bridge between goals and achievement. It separates winners and losers as can be seen in the Fable of the Tortoise and the Hare.

In this story, the rabbit knows that he is faster than the turtle, so he takes a nap in the middle of the race. Meanwhile, with self-discipline, the turtle continues to trudge along, and eventually manages to arrive first at the finish line. Like the turtle, with self-discipline, you can finish what you start doing.

Self-Discipline enables you to choose, and then persevere with actions, thoughts, and behaviors that lead to improvement and success. Nikola Tesla has said that "he could only achieve success in life through self-discipline, and he applied it until his will and his wish became one."

Self-Discipline creates confidence and self-mastery, and gives you freedom and self-control.

Self-Discipline leads to success.

The Power of Optimism

THE DISPOSITION OR TENDENCY TO LOOK ON THE MORE FAVORABLE SIDE OF EVENTS OR CONDITIONS AND TO EXPECT THE MOST FAVORABLE OUTCOMES.

"When life hands you lemons, make lemonade."
— UNKNOWN

Optimism is the ability to see the world in a positive light. Thinking positively can improve the outcome of events and help you to cope with less than desirable circumstances. It can help you to commit to goals, work on them, and achieve them. It builds resilience, inspires, and unites. Being optimistic can make you happier, improve your self-esteem and confidence. Your health can benefit from it. Studies have shown that optimism can reduce stress and anxiety and lengthen life. By simply having a positive view on life, both your physical and mental health will prosper.

Difficulties in life are experienced by everyone. Optimists are proactive. They deal with prospects. Baseball player, Pete Rose once said: "Every time I step up to the plate, I expect to get a hit. If I don't expect to get a hit, I have no right to step into the batter's box in the first place. It is a positive expectation that has gotten me all of the hits in my career." (Pete Rose holds Major League baseball's record for the most hits at 4,256.)

An old story about identical twins rings home the power of positivity and optimism. One twin was an optimist and the other was a pessimist They each received a gift. The pessimist got a new computer. However, he was unhappy and complained that he did not like the color of the computer. The optimist got a box or manure. He was excited and said that with this much manure, there must be a pony somewhere.

Positive things happen to positive people.

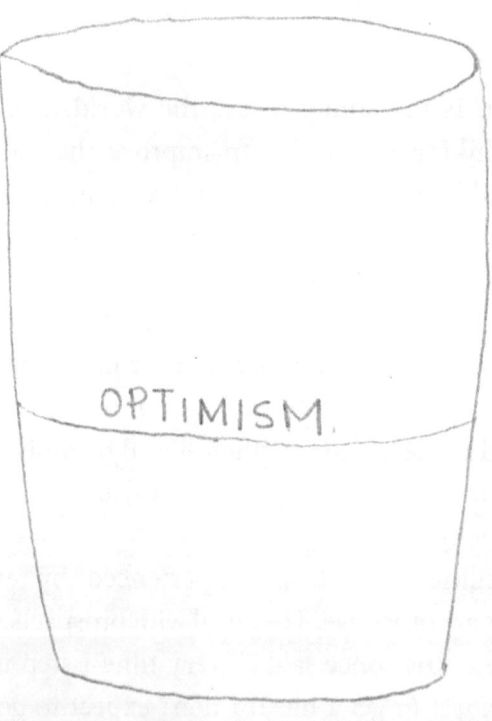

The Power of Effort

A VIGOROUS DETERMINED ATTEMPT: TRYING

> "The credit goes to the man in the arena whose face is covered by dust and sweat and blood; who strives valiantly; who at best knows the triumph of high achievement, and who at worst fails while daring greatly, so that his place shall never be with those cold and timid souls who neither know the ecstasy of victory nor the agony of defeat."
> — TEDDY ROOSEVELT

Effort paves the way to success, keeps us focused, teaches us that we can do more than we think we can, and gives us new skills and abilities. Author Mark Wiggins tells us that: "Mental toughness with extreme effort is the formula for success."

Many years ago, I had the good fortune to coach a youth volleyball team that was in the highest division in our region. I also noticed that a team in the lowest division was coached by an outstanding athlete and player from Japan who I had competed against. His team repeatedly won divisional tournaments and kept moving up to higher divisions. I knew one of the athletes who played for him, and I asked what was causing this consistent improvement. Was it new tactics, motivational talks, or skill improvement? The young athlete said no, and could not think of anything that created this improvement. The athlete went on to say that it was very difficult to understand what the coach said because he had a very heavy accent. In fact, he said the coach mostly repeated one word over and over--- "Try, Try, Try." (So simple) As Vince Lombardi said: "Effort is everything."

Soo... Try, Try, Try!

The Power of the Truth and Honesty

THAT WHICH IS IN ACCORDANCE WITH
FACT OR REALITY: INTEGRITY

"Honesty is the Best Policy"
— EDWIN SANDYS

There once was a poor woodcutter who was a good man and worked very hard. One day while chopping down a tree, his axe slipped out of his hands and fell into a river. He searched and searched, but could not find it. Totally dejected, he sat down on the riverbank. An angel appeared and promised to help him find his axe. The angel dove into the river and retrieved an axe that was completely made of gold. The man said that it wasn't his axe and refused to accept it. The angel dove again and returned with a silver axe, but the woodcutter refused again explaining that his was made of steel. The angel went into the river for one last time and returned with the steel axe. The man thanked the angel profusely. Impressed by his honesty, the angel told the woodcutter to keep both the gold and the silver axe.

Dishonesty is a surprisingly easy way to throw away your freedom. It results in you not being trusted, being worried, anxious and always on guard for fear of losing what you have gained.

On the other hand, when you are known to be honest and truthful, others accept you at your word and are able to relax around you. You are more relaxed because you have nothing to hide. You are free to say what you think and to mean what you say. You know that you have earned what you have. You are also free to share your innermost thoughts. Being truthful leads to a better quality of life and has positive mental and physical effects. It gives you a clear conscience, a good reputation, and better sleep, confidence, and pride.

"*And the Truth Shall Set You Free*" — JOHN 8:32

The Power of Belief

ACCEPTING THAT SOMETHING IS
TRUE OR REAL

*"Believe that life is worth living and
your belief will create the fact."*
— WILLIAM JAMES

Author Seth Adam Smith has written that "without faith, you are as a crow that has forgotten his ability to fly; you peck at the dark muddy earth when the bright mountains lie before you." Your belief determines your action, and your action determines the result.

This is reinforced by the story about a man at an elephant camp who noticed that those huge animals were only restrained by a small piece of rope tied to one leg and to a pole pegged into the ground. These giant beasts could have easily broken free and escaped. The man questioned why they didn't break free. He was told that when they were very young that the rope was strong enough to restrain them. It conditioned them to believe that is wasn't possible to escape so they didn't try when they got older and stronger.

Author Dennis Waitley has said that "if you believe you can, you probably will. If you believe you can't, you most assuredly won't. Belief is the ignition switch that gets you off the launching pad." People who achieved success believed with all their hearts that they could do it. In order to accomplish things, we must believe.

Believing gives living purpose and life meaning. It empowers us and motivates us to do better, to get better, and to try better.

Believing that you can be successful is the most important step in actually achieving. What you believe you eventually become, and that determines how you experience the world. You are what you believe you are. Belief gives you unlimited power.

Believe that you can.

The Power of Intensity

EMPLOYING GREAT STRENGTH OR FORCE

"Intensity gets results."
— JAMES TERRY

In order to be successful, your focus must be so intense that people may think you are crazy. The focus must take the form of extreme concentration, energy, drive, passion and burning desire. You must feel deeply, sincerely, and willfully. You don't waste time and you plan to win. You go the extra mile.

While one person might just coast by without much effort, the intense one will study, practice , and take advantage of every opportunity to reach a goal. For example, when exercising at a sufficient intensity, the body builds endurance and strength.

The world needs intense people who can find new directions, invent new things, support the spontaneous, and be big picture thinkers. They inspire and create momentum. Their most distinguishing characteristic is their intensity of purpose. They attack what is in front of them with passion and purpose without fear or doubt and without an ounce of quit. They push until they succeed.

Use intensity to reach your goals.

The Power of Hope

A FEELING OF TRUST, OPTIMISM, DESIRE, AND AN EXPECTATION THAT A CERTAIN THING WILL HAPPEN

"Hope is a companion of power and mother of success."
— SAMUEL SMILES

This is seen in a story about a hospital teacher who was asked to work with a young boy in the burn unit. When she met the boy who was badly burned and in great pain, she told him that she was there to help him with his school work.

The boy's condition had been deteriorating because he had given up hope, but after meeting the teacher his whole attitude changed, and he started to respond to treatment.

Why the big change? With tears in his eyes, the boy said that he thought that he was going to die until he met the teacher. He then realized that the hospital would not have sent a teacher to work with a dying boy.

Hope does lead to positive results. It helps you face anything in life with confidence. Hope builds up your faith and promotes change. It sparks you to push through challenges.

Actor Christopher Reeve has said that "once you choose hope anything is possible." Charles Dickens wrote that: "hope is the last thing ever lost—Hope, Hope to the last." Don't give up on hope. Keep on trying until you reach your goal.

Where there is life there is hope.

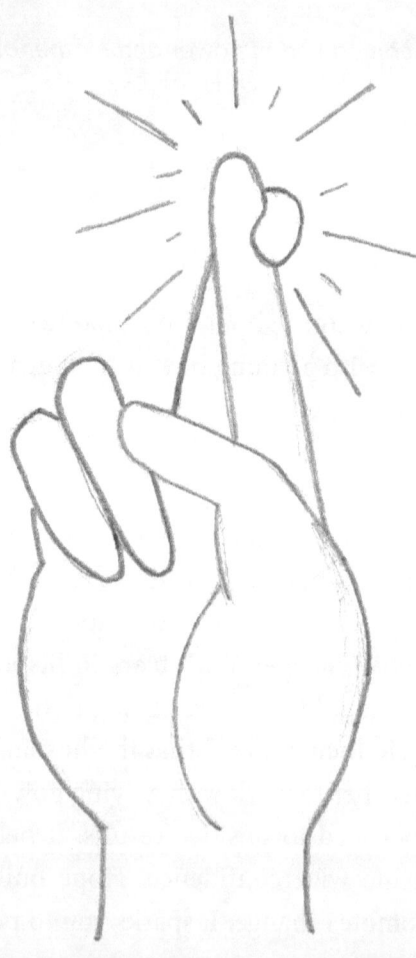

The Power of Diligence

THE STEADY, EARNEST, AND ENERGETIC EFFORT TO ACCOMPLISH A GIVEN TASK OR GOAL

"What we hope ever to do with ease, we must first learn to do with diligence."
— SAMUEL JOHNSON

Diligence is where you invest your whole energy to complete a task or reach a goal. You do not give up; you stay committed to your goals. You use available resources and opportunities to get results. Diligence is important to you because it uses commitment to transform your vision into reality.

An example of this is the tale of two caterpillars building their cocoons. After a few days, one stopped, but the other kept working. Eventually the diligent one entered the cocoon and later emerged as a beautiful butterfly and flew away. The lazy one remained a caterpillar, and was sad and angry because it had missed something wonderful simply because it was not willing to work hard.

Diligence allows you to adapt and change and become resilient to obstacles along the way. It helps you to see beyond struggles and sacrifices and to focus on the end result.

Give it all to get it all.

The Power of Resilience

THE ABILITY TO WORK THROUGH
AND TO BOUNCE BACK FROM
DIFFICULT PROBLEMS AND KEEP ON GOING

*"Our greatest weakness lies in giving up.
The most certain way to succeed is
always to try just one more time."*
— THOMAS EDISON

Resilience is the ability to get backup when you are knocked down. It is the ability to recover from stress, catastrophe, illness, depression, and adversity. Resilience makes you more positive and optimistic and strengthens your ability to regulate your emotions. It helps you to stay the course through the most trying circumstances. Resilience makes you stronger. It helps you remain stable and calm and able to cope with stress. Resilience is a skill that must be developed, and it is a key to you having a happy and healthy life.

Resilience is how you recharge, not how you endure.

Nature tells us that the river is stronger than the mountain. It finds paths around obstacles and sometimes even creates new paths. In nature, water cuts rocks.

Thus resilience helps us change or redirect for success. Resilience is resourceful, adaptable, creative and flexible and gives us the energy and capacity to change.

Resilience finds a way.

The Power of Experience

HAVING BEEN AFFECTED BY OR
GAINED KNOWLEDGE THROUGH
DIRECT OBSERVATION OR PARTICIPATION

"We are the sum of our experiences."
— B.J. NEBLETT

Once an unskilled woman was hired by a large company to do low level work at minimum wage. Every day she had to commute for one hour each way to get to and from work. To say the least, this was exhausting, and there seemed to be no end in sight. A friend told her that in order to improve her opportunities, she needed to acquire marketable and needed skills. But how could she find the time? A thought came to her, and she bought some language tapes with the goal of learning Spanish. She listened to the tapes daily on her two hour commute. Within two years, she became proficient in Spanish. She then purchased new tapes, and worked with them for three years and mastered Japanese.

At that point, her company went international, and opened a new position for a person who was fluent in Spanish and Japanese. The woman applied for the job, was the only applicant who qualified and got the job. With it came a six figure salary, a company car, an expense account, and international travel. Having experience with the company and the skills that were needed, transformed her life.

Experience helps you learn. It shapes what you know and strengthens your relationships with others and changes your perceptions. It allows you to learn from your mistakes, and to hopefully better yourself in the future. Experience helps you grow as an individual, and it shapes your personality, your motives, and your outlook on life. Experience makes you more understanding, independent, and self-confident. It helps you know what to expect, be more engaged, and be more productive. Experience enhances your skills and showcases your talents. It shows that you are capable, and earns you respect because "you have been there and done that."

Motivational speaker Haley Hobson points out that : "Without experience, there will never be true knowledge," and author Benny Lewis tells us that : "Experience is the greatest teacher of all." In short, experience is one of the most powerful exposures in life.

Experience is a key to becoming successful.

The Power of Laughter
A SHOWING OF POSITIVE EMOTION

"When you awaken love and laughter in your life, your mind lets go of fear and anxiety and your happy spirit becomes the healing balm that transforms every aspect of your human experience."
— JESSE DYLAN

It has been said that laughter is the best medicine. Laughter makes you feel better by lessening stress, anxiety, depression and even blood pressure. At the same time, it improves memory. Socially, laughter removes the distance and walls between people, improving them emotionally and mentally, recharging them and bringing them closer together.

When giving a presentation, a joke or a funny anecdote can win over your audience. It makes you more approachable, and can help you make a good first impression and put people at ease. It is a mood booster that relaxes you, and can lead to greater opportunities for success.

Enjoy: An older man went to his clinic for a checkup. The examination and labs showed that everything was fine, especially for a man of his age. For his age he asked: "I am only 80. Do you think that I can make it to 90?" The clinician asked, "Do you drink or smoke or eat fatty meats and sweets or engage in risky activities?" The man said of course not! The clinician thought for a moment, and then asked: "Why in the world would you want to live to 90?"

Make it a habit to laugh every day.

The Power of Talent and Skills

THE POWER OF TALENT
NATURAL ABILITY OR POWER

"Real Talent Shows Through."
— PABMA FAITH

Talent is a natural ability and a gift that creates opportunity and gives you an advantage. Your talents predispose you to succeed in certain areas. They give you a clue to your purpose, and are your greatest source of power and personal energy. They allow you to reach your full potential.

It has been said that talent wins over a learned skill. However, this is not always true. Talent can be a double-edged sword. High school basketball coach, Tim Notke, cautions us that: "Hard work beats talent when talent fails to work hard. "Nothing is more common than unsuccessful men with talent.

Those who are talented sometimes fail to recognize the importance of hard work along with developing their own natural abilities. In order for talents to really shine, they need to be linked to passion. The discipline to perform the skill has to be there or talents will never be fully utilized nor will they ever be fully realized. Thus talent is a key to success, but only if you work hard to develop it.

As a coach, I have seen scenarios where one athlete relies solely on native ability and only becomes a very good performer, but never maximizes his talent.

Use it or lose it.

On the other hand, I have seen other athletes without special talents who through desire, effort, and hard work have developed their skills and techniques immensely to the point that they have become truly outstanding. This leads to our next power.

The Power of Skills

ACQUIRED ABILITIES THAT COME FROM TRAINING, EXPERIENCE, OR PRACTICE

"The future belongs to those who learn new skills and combine them in creative ways."
— ROBERT GREENE

Skills require practice and work. They are the building blocks to goal achievement. A winner is someone who recognizes his ability, works his tail off to improve and perfect his skills and techniques, and uses them to accomplish a goal. They give one a better chance to succeed. They enhance life. Professor of psychology and author, Angela Duckworth, presents a formula that posits:

Ability x Effort = Skill
Skill x Effort = Achievement

Your skills showcase the best in you. Skills that you acquire lead to success, and the more time and energy that you put into practice of what you are trying to achieve, the closer you come to skill mastery. In daily life, skills exhibit their power. Obstacles that you face are overcome by the skills that you have developed. So, skills are simply the things that you learn that enable you to successfully perform tasks.

*It's not what you have that counts;
it's what you do with what you have that counts.*

The Power of Caring

THE ACT OF DISPLAYING KINDNESS AND CONCERN FOR OTHERS

"You can really change the world if you care enough."
— MARILYN WRIGHT EDELMAN

Caring must be shared to be effective.

This can be seen in a story about an ant that one day fell into a stream and was about to drown. A dove sitting on a tree saw this, and plucked a leaf, and dropped it into the stream close to the ant. The ant climbed onto it and floated safely to the bank of the stream. Later, the ant saw a man preparing to throw a net over the dove and capture it. Seeing this, the ant started biting the man on the foot. The man yelled causing the bird to fly away to safety.

It is amazing what a little caring can do, and it is amazing the long term affects that it can have.

Empathy connects you to others. It builds relationships and it creates happiness. It makes you happy.

Be caring.

The Power of Gratitude

BEING THANKFUL AND APPRECIATIVE

"Be thankful for what you have and you'll end up having more. If you concentrate on what you don't have, you'll never have enough."
— OPRAH WINFREY

Gratitude increases your happiness and decreases your depression. An attitude of gratitude creates a positive mindset the brings more positivity into your life. It can actually improve your health and well-being. Author Eckhart Tolle tells us that: "Acknowledging the good that you already have in your life is the foundation of all abundance." It turns jobs into joy and changes ordinary opportunities into blessings.

This can be seen in the story of a lady who worked faithfully as a janitor for twenty years without ever receiving a thank-you. Her company soon changed owners. Within a few days the new owner wrote a personal thank you card to every employee in the company. He had his assistant go around and hand them out.

When the lady received her card, she burst into tears. When friends asked her what was wrong, she said that she was really touched by the card of gratitude. In fact she had actually been thinking of quitting when the ownership changed, but this little bit of effort by the new owner changed everything. Gratitude is powerful indeed.

Have an attitude of gratitude.

The Power of Courage

THE ABILITY TO DO SOMETHING
THAT FRIGHTENS YOU

*"Courage in not the absence of fear,
but the triumph over it."*
— NELSON MANDELLA

A shy and cowardly person went to a martial arts master and asked him to teach him courage. The master told him to go to a big city, and tell everyone that he met that he was a coward. This frightened the man, and at first he could not do it. He persisted despite his fear. The task became easier every day until he realized that he was not afraid anymore. When his task was done, he returned to his master and thanked him saying that he was not afraid anymore. He then asked: How did the master know that the task would work? The master told him that cowardice is only a habit. By doing things that frightened him he was able to break the habit. Courage is also a habit. In order to develop it, he needed to move into the fear. That is when fear goes away, and bravery and courage take its place.

Courage helps you overcome obstacles and achieve goals. It gives you confidence in your abilities. It causes you to act according to you values rather than your impulses.

It is contagious. Courage pushes you out of your comfort zone and gives you the ability to do what is necessary. It allows you to triumph over fear, and it gives you control over your life. Courage shows you that you are far more powerful than you think you are.

Develop the habit of courage.

The Power of Expectancy

THE FEELING THAT SOMETHING WILL HAPPEN

> *"The more you expect from life, the more your expectations will be fulfilled.*
> — DEAN KOONTE

In the 1970s, the *National Geographic* ran an article entitled "The Centenarians." It studied several places in different parts of the world that had pockets of centenarians. The study searched for common factors that led to the health and longevity of these people. Surprisingly, the researchers found that diet and exercise were not common factors. However, they did find psychological factors that these people did have in common. Two of these were that they had something that they had to do and that they were respected. However, the one thing that they had most in common was that they all expected to be healthy and to live to be over one hundred years old.

Dennis Waitley in his *Psychology of Winning* says that winners expect to win, and that mental obsessions have physical manifestations. In the long run, you receive what you expect. In short, you program your subconscious to reach your goal. You get what you set and you get what you expect.

You get what you expect.

The Power of Endurance
THE ABILITY TO WITHSTAND HARDSHIP OR ADVERSITY FOR A LONG TIME

> *"Come what may, all bad fortune is to be conquered by endurance."*
> — VIRGIL

Endurance creates strength and builds stamina and empowers you. It lets you outlast your opponents. It allows you to forget about everything else and withstand almost anything until your goal is attained.

This can be seen in the story of Juliane Koepek. The plane in which she was flying came apart in mid-air over Peru, and plunged 10,000 feet and crashed into the jungle. The seventeen year-old girl was the sole survivor. When she regained consciousness, she had a broken collar bone and maggot infested wounds. Undaunted, she walked and swam for ten days with vultures circling over her head until she found help.

Her endurance and abilities had been tested to the limit. She had stayed calm, kept moving, and had ignored the pain. Juliane had refused to give-in despite her horrific situation.

Endurance plays a critical role in our survival, and in achieving our goals and dreams.

Endurance Conquers All.

The Power of Teamwork

THE ABILITY TO WORK TOGETHER
TOWARD A COMMON GOAL

*"If everyone is moving forward, then
success takes care of itself."*
— HENRY FORD

The whole is greater than the sum of its parts. In other words, one might be able to accomplish a task as an individual, but would be able to accomplish much more as a team, and do it sooner. Good teamwork requires a group of people who participate, have open communication, mutually treat and respect each other, and most importantly have common goals.

Once a manager had a forty person team composed of bright, enthusiastic, and hardworking people. Individually, everyone was excelling, but as a team, they were not good. He decided to solve the problem with a "Team Building Game" that consisted of three rounds. In the first round they were taken into a room, told to take a balloon in the room, blow it up and write their name on it, and then to leave the room. In the second round, hundreds of inflated balloons along with the team's balloons were scattered around the room. They were give ten minutes to find their own balloons, and that the first three to do so would win. Everyone searched, but no one found their balloon in time. In the third round there were told that if they found a balloon with a name on it, they had to give it to that person. Within a few minutes everyone had their own balloon. The manager pointed out that they had failed in the second round because they had acted as individuals, but that they had succeeded in the third round because of sharing and teamwork.

Teamwork increases your efficiency, it builds your confidence, improves your communication skills, makes you accountable, and gives you direction. It commits you to a goal and teaches you how to accept responsibility. It also reduces your stress. A team is only as good as its weakest member. Commitment to a goal, the participation and effort of each member, and proper role assignments that complement each other's strengths are critical to the team's success.

The strength of the team is each individual member and the strength of each member is the team.

The Power of Commitment

THE DEDICATION TO A CAUSE OR GOAL

> *"The quality of a person's life is in direct proportion to his commitment to excellence regardless of his chosen field of endeavor."*
> — VINCE LOMBARDI

Once a farmer was very good to a pig and a chicken on his farm, and they wanted to do something nice for him. The chicken suggested that the farmer would enjoy a ham and egg breakfast. The chicken went on to say that it could provide the eggs, but where would they get the ham? The pig acknowledged that the chicken was making a fine contribution, but that the pig would have to make a real commitment.

Commitment leads to action and commitment leads to achievement. It gets you to do whatever it takes to reach your goal. It transforms a promise into reality. If you are committed, you know who you are, what you want, and what you have to do to get it. You are open and frank and have values.

Commitment gets results.

The Power of Consistency

DEDICATING YOURSELF TO YOUR GOALS AND STAYING FOCUSED ON THE THINGS AND ACTIVITIES NEEDED TO ACHIEVE THEM

"It's not what you do once in a while that shapes your life. It's what you do consistently."
— ANTHONY ROBBINS

Author Jim Collins reminds us of the difficult process of relentlessly pushing a large, heavy flywheel, turn by turn, very slowly building speed until it starts to turn with much less effort, spinning faster and faster, with less and less effort.

A series of well-executed, consistent efforts create a powerful cumulative effect. Consistency is the foundation of trust, respect, and success. It shows that what counts is showing up and working relentlessly until a goal is achieved. Consistency outlasts the lucky and outlasts the lazy. It leads to growth, discipline, and momentum. It builds self-confidence and self-control. It contributes to efficiency.

Consistency is a key to success.

The Power of Love

AN INTENSE FEELING OF
DEEP AFFECTION AND CARING;
A GIFT WITHOUT EXPECTATIONS,
CONDITIONS OR LIMITATIONS

"It's love that makes the world go round."
— W.S. GILBERT

Love is a basic emotion, and the most precious gift in the world. It gives you strength and courage, and it creates positive connections with others for you. It is powerful enough to alter your mindset and enhance your relationships and communication. It is powerful enough to empower you to do great things and become a better person. Love opens you to others and creates happiness. You care for another's happiness as much as you care for your own.

Many years ago a little girl was suffering from a rare disease. Her only chance of recovery was a blood transfusion from her younger five-year old brother, who had miraculously survived the same disease and had developed antibodies that would combat his sister's illness. The doctor explained the situation to the little boy, and asked him if he would be willing to give his blood to his sister. He hesitated for only a moment before taking a deep breath and saying that he would do it to save her life. As the transfusion progressed, the color started returning to the girl's cheeks. But the boy's face grew pale and his smile faded. He looked up to the doctor and asked in a trembling voice if he would start to die right away. Being so young, the little boy misunderstood and thought that he was going to have to give all of his blood and die in order to save his sister.

Author Stephen Kindrick tells us that: "The only way love can last a lifetime is if it is unconditional. Love is that condition in which the happiness of another person is essential to your own."

Be a lover!

The Power of Fulfillment

A FEELING THAT YOUR ABILITIES ARE
BEING FULLY USED AND FELT AND
ARE CARRYING TO FRUITION
YOUR DEEPEST DESIRES

"Fulfillment leads inwardly to the guarantee of peace"
— RASHEED OGUNLARA

Fulfillment allows you to pursue things that matter to you and that you are passionate about. Your true merit in life is measured by how much you have mattered to others, by making a difference in the lives of others. Living a life that matters gives you a sense of meaning and purpose. It gives significance and worth to your life. It shows that you have figured out what you love to do and have made it your life's work.

The results are that it makes you happy, confident, joyful, and it connects you to others. It makes you comfortable with who you are and what you are doing and have done. Fulfillment increases your sense of inner well-being and gives you a feeling of great satisfaction and a sense of completion. It makes you feel that you have reached your full potential.

Fulfillment is when you have achieved peace and happiness through what you have done in your daily life.

Seek Fulfillment.

Final Thoughts

As you finish reading this book, I hope that by identifying some of the "Powers" that resonate with you that you will be able to eliminate the words entitled, deserved, owed, victim, and powerless from your vocabulary. I also hope that by utilizing those powers that they will lead you to the achievement of all of your personal goals, and that therein you will find success, happiness, satisfaction, fulfillment, and freedom. Remember, you have to earn it to deserve it.

You are in control of your destiny.

Special Thanks

My teaching colleague and friend, Paula Fox gets a special thanks for her efforts editing this book, and for making it more readable for you.

It has been said that a picture is worth a thousand words. So special thanks also go to my daughter, Teri D'Arcy for her artwork that definitely enhances this book.

Finally, a special thanks to my wife, Sharkie, for her encouragement, support and expertise, and also for typing the original rough draft and final manuscript.

Much Love

www.ingramcontent.com/pod-product-compliance
Lightning Source LLC
Chambersburg PA
CBHW030454010526
44118CB00011B/928